U.S.A. TRAVEL GUIDES

MICHIGAN

BY ANN HEINRICHS • ILLUSTRATED BY MATT KANIA

The Child's World®
childsworld.com

Published by The Child's World®
1980 Lookout Drive • Mankato, MN 56003-1705
800-599-READ • www.childsworld.com

ISBN 9781503819627
LCCN 2016961175

Printing
Printed in the United States of America
PA02334

Ann Heinrichs is the author of more than 100 books for children and young adults. She has also enjoyed successful careers as a children's book editor and an advertising copywriter. Ann grew up in Fort Smith, Arkansas, and lives in Chicago, Illinois.

About the Author
Ann Heinrichs

Matt Kania loves maps and, as a kid, dreamed of making them. In school he studied geography and cartography, and today he makes maps for a living. Matt's favorite thing about drawing maps is learning about the places they represent. Many of the maps he has created can be found in books, magazines, videos, Web sites, and public places.

About the
Map Illustrator
Matt Kania

On the cover: Holland, Michigan is famous for its historic windmills and its springtime tulip festival.

OUR MICHIGAN TRIP

MICHIGAN

What a trip's in store for you! You're about to tour Michigan.

You'll go snowmobiling and saw a log. You'll travel deep underground into a mine. You'll watch trucks being made and learn about the history of the automobile. You'll listen to Motown music. You'll learn about Henry Ford and the Supremes. So what do you say? Shall we hit the road? Then buckle up, and hang on tight. We're off!

WELCOME TO MICHIGAN

Isle Royale

LAKE SUPERIOR

Keweenaw Peninsula

CANADA

Michigan's Nicknames: The Wolverine State, the Great Lakes State, and the Water Wonderland

Pictured Rocks National Lakeshore

Sault Sainte Marie

Iron Mountain

Tahquamenon Falls

Mackinaw City

As you travel through Michigan, watch for all the interesting facts along the way.

WISCONSIN

Grayling

LAKE HURON

MICHIGAN

Cadillac

Cass City

LAKE MICHIGAN

Mt. Pleasant

Chippewa River

75

69

Holland

96

Lansing

Hickory Corners

Dearborn

Detroit

94

69

Eau Claire

LAKE ERIE

INDIANA

OHIO

Highest Temperature: Mio and Stanwood July 13, 1936 112°F (44°C)

Lowest Temperature: Vanderbilt February 9, 1934 -51°F (-46°C)

LAKE SUPERIOR

Upper Peninsula

Mount Arvon

Pictured Rocks National Lakeshore

CANADA

Tahquamenon Falls

Straits of Mackinac

Here we are in the UP. No, not UP as in "up and down." UP stands for "Upper Peninsula"!

Vanderbilt

Empire

Mio

LAKE HURON

WISCONSIN

Stanwood

Lower Peninsula

How much water goes over Tahquamenon Falls? On the Upper Falls, it's more than 50,000 gallons (189,271 L) of water a second. That would fill up about 1,000 bathtubs!

LAKE MICHIGAN

Lake Ontario is the only Great Lake not touching Michigan.

HIGHEST AND LOWEST POINTS HIGHEST: Mount Arvon at 1,979 feet (603 m) LOWEST: Along Lake Erie at 572 feet (174 m)

Pictured Rocks National Lakeshore is on Lake Superior. It has colorful and unusually shaped cliffs.

Sleeping Bear Dunes National Lakeshore is near Empire. Its tall sand dunes rise above Lake Michigan.

OHIO

LAKE ERIE

TAHQUAMENON FALLS ON THE UPPER PENINSULA

Tahquamenon Falls makes a roaring, thundering sound. Ojibwe Native Americans settled near these falls in the 1500s. Later, loggers began to arrive in the late 1800s. They sent their logs tumbling down the waterfall.

Michigan has lots of waterfalls, rivers, and lakes. Four of the country's Great Lakes border Michigan. They are Lake Superior, Lake Michigan, Lake Huron, and Lake Erie.

Michigan has two main sections of land. In the north is the Upper **Peninsula**. That's where Tahquamenon Falls is located. The Lower Peninsula is in the south. It's shaped like a mitten!

The Upper and Lower Peninsulas don't touch each other. A narrow waterway runs between them. It's called the **Straits** of Mackinac.

The Upper Tahquamenon Falls is one of the largest waterfalls east of the Mississippi River.

WATCHING WILDLIFE ALONG THE CHIPPEWA RIVER

Have you ever watched wildlife from a canoe? The Chippewa River is great for viewing wildlife. And Mount Pleasant is a perfect place to start. Just launch your canoe from the nature park there. Soon you'll be drifting along the river's shady banks.

You'll see deer with their new fawns. You might also spot wild turkeys nearby. If it's very quiet, you'll see beavers, too. Blue herons are along the banks. Hawks and eagles soar high in the sky.

Forests cover more than half of Michigan. The state also has thousands of rivers and streams. That's why it's called the Water Wonderland.

You might see deer or geese if you venture into Michigan's wilderness.

STATE FLOWER
APPLE BLOSSOM

STATE TREE
WHITE PINE

STATE BIRD
AMERICAN ROBIN

Look! There's a beaver! Here's a wild turkey! There's a fawn!

LAKE SUPERIOR

CANADA

LAKE HURON

WISCONSIN

Chippewa River

Mount Pleasant

LAKE MICHIGAN

More than 1,700,000 white-tailed deer live in Michigan.

The National Park Service has seven sites in Michigan.

INDIANA

OHIO

LAKE ERIE

Native Americans built huge mounds of earth near Grand Rapids. The mounds were used as burial sites.

Who Lived Here before Europeans Arrived? Chippewa (Ojibwe), Menominee, Miami, Ottawa (Odawa), Potawatomi, and Wyandot

LAKE SUPERIOR

CANADA

• Sault Sainte Marie

WISCONSIN

LAKE HURON

I see a carving of a water panther. It protects the waters of the Great Lakes.

• Cass City

LAKE MICHIGAN

• Grand Rapids

Sault Sainte Marie was Michigan's first permanent European settlement. A priest named Father Jacques Marquette founded it in 1668.

More than 50,000 Native Americans live in Michigan today.

Explorer Étienne Brulé arrived in present-day Michigan in about 1620. He may have been the first European in the area.

THE SANILAC PETROGLYPHS IN CASS CITY

You are walking on smooth sandstone. Around you, you see shapes and symbols carved into the stone. Native Americans carved these images between 300 and 1,000 years ago. These carvings are called petroglyphs. You are at the Sanilac Petroglyphs in Cass City.

The Sanilac Petroglyphs are sacred to the Native American tribes of the Great Lakes Region. The petroglyphs were likely carved by their **ancestors**. Each petroglyph has a meaning. An archer shoots knowledge into the future. A giant bird called the thunderbird controls the weather.

The first European settlers came to present-day Michigan in the 1660s. They were French explorers from Canada. French trappers and traders later followed. Roman Catholic priests came, too. They hoped to **convert** the Native Americans to Christianity.

A visitor studies the Sanilac Petroglyphs in Cass City, Michigan.

A fur trader counts his animal skins. A soldier stands guard nearby. A woman cooks dinner over an open fire. You'll see them all at Colonial Michilimackinac in Mackinaw City.

Michilimackinac was a fur-trading post and army fort. French traders built it in 1715. Furs were a big business in this region. The forests were full of furry animals. Both the French and Native Americans such as the Ojibwe trapped them. They traded animal skins at the trading posts.

Great Britain won Michigan from France in 1763. After that, Michilimackinac became a British fort. Michigan soon changed hands again. American colonists beat the British in the Revolutionary War (1775–1783). Michigan became part of the United States in 1837.

The buildings in Fort Michilimackinac were reconstructed based on historic maps.

During Pontiac's Rebellion (1763), Ottawa chief Pontiac captured some British posts.

Beaver furs were used to make hats and coats.

LAKE SUPERIOR

CANADA

Bang! Pow! Kaboom! They're showing how the soldiers used to fire cannons and guns.

Mackinac Island

Straits of Mackinac

Mackinaw City

WISCONSIN

LAKE HURON

France and Great Britain fought each other in North America. This conflict is called the French and Indian War (1754-1763). Great Britain won. Then, Great Britain took over most of France's land in North America.

River Raisin Battlefield is in Monroe. This battle between British and American troops took place on January 22, 1813. It was part of the War of 1812 (1812–1815).

Detroit

Antoine de la Mothe, Sieur de Cadillac, built Fort Pontchartrain in 1701. It eventually became the city of Detroit.

Historic Fort Mackinac is on Mackinac Island in the Straits of Mackinac. British soldiers built it in the late 1700s.

Monroe

LAKE ERIE

OHIO

Michigan was the 26th state to enter the Union. It joined on January 26, 1837.

LAKE SUPERIOR

CANADA

Keweenaw Peninsula

• Negaunee

Upper Peninsula

• Iron Mountain

The Iron Mountain mine operated from 1870 to 1945.

WISCONSIN

LAKE HURON

Those logs are huge! They kept the mine roof from caving in. Mining sounds pretty dangerous.

LAKE MICHIGAN

Iron was found near present-day Negaunee in 1844.

The commercial mining of copper began on the Keweenaw Peninsula in 1843. Keweenaw National Historical Park preserves sites from the mining days.

The Library of Michigan opened in Detroit in 1828.

Detroit •

LAKE ERIE

OHIO

TOURING THE MINE AT IRON MOUNTAIN

Put on your hard hat. Then hop aboard the train. You're heading deep underground. How deep? Four hundred feet (122 m)! You're touring an iron mine at Iron Mountain. You'll see how miners used to work down there. They wore hard hats, too.

The Upper Peninsula is rich in iron **ore**. People began mining there in the 1840s. Copper was discovered there at about the same time. Thousands of people rushed in for mining jobs.

All over Michigan, **pioneers** were making new homes. Many were **immigrants** from European lands. Everyone was looking for a better life.

A train carries iron from a Michigan iron mine in the late 1800s.

THE TULIP TIME FESTIVAL IN HOLLAND

Clack, clack, thunk! Those dancers sure make a lot of noise. But that's not surprising— they're wearing wooden shoes!

It's the Tulip Time Festival in Holland. Lots of people are wearing **traditional** Dutch costumes. That includes *klompen*, or wooden shoes.

A group of immigrants settled here in 1847. Most were Dutch people. They came from the Netherlands. One region of the Netherlands is called Holland. The immigrants named Holland, Michigan, after their homeland. The Dutch are famous for their tulips. So the townspeople of Holland began planting them. They bloom during the festival.

How well can you dance in wooden shoes? Find out at the Tulip Time Festival!

In 2016, 9,928,300 people lived in Michigan. It's the tenth-largest state by population.

More than 500,000 people from 40 countries come to this festival each year.

LAKE SUPERIOR

CANADA

WISCONSIN

LAKE HURON

LAKE MICHIGAN

• Grand Rapids
• Holland

Warren •
• Detroit

LAKE ERIE

OHIO

Population of Largest Cities
Detroit.............................677,116
Grand Rapids................195,097
Warren............................135,358

Many immigrants settled in Michigan. They came from the Netherlands, England, Ireland, Germany, Poland, and many other countries.

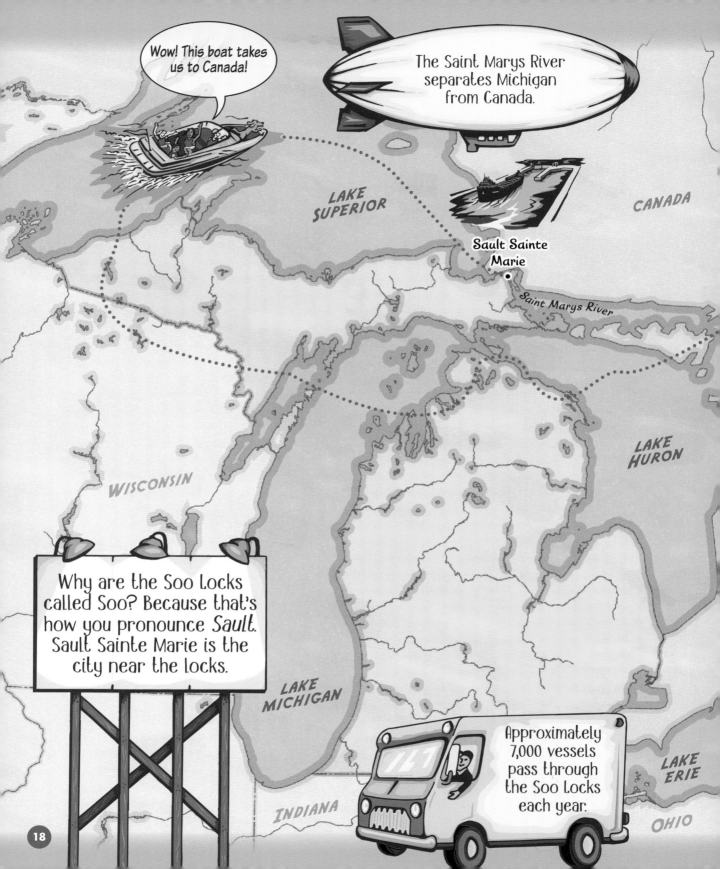

THE SOO LOCKS BOAT TOUR

Your boat glides through a gate. The gate shuts and locks tight. Another gate opens, and water rushes in. The water lifts your boat two stories higher. Then you sail into Lake Superior.

You're touring the Soo Locks. The State of Michigan built this passage in 1855 to solve a shipping problem. In the 1800s, iron and other goods were produced along Lake Superior. But how could people ship those goods?

The Saint Marys River seemed like a good route. It flows from Lake Superior to Lake Huron. From there, boats could travel far and wide. But the river had a big waterfall. People dug a **canal** around the falls. They built locks to raise and lower water levels. Then boats could move up and down!

All aboard! Learn about Michigan's freight shipping history when you tour the Soo Locks.

Have you ever seen a two-person saw? It's long, with handles on both ends. One person grabs each handle. Then they lean back and forth to saw. That's how people used to saw logs.

You can try it yourself at Wood Shaving Days. This festival takes place at Hartwick Pines State Park. It celebrates Michigan's logging days. You'll see wood-carvers and blacksmiths. There's a steam-powered sawmill, too.

Logging became a big **industry** in the late 1800s. Loggers lived in logging camps. They cut down trees and sawed huge logs. Then they floated the logs down a river. The logs arrived at a sawmill. There they were sawed into flat boards. People built homes and stores with this wood.

Detroit loggers stand atop a giant log in the late 1800s.

Detroit is called the Motor City. Some people just call it Motown!

Dear Mr. Ford:
You decided to make cars on an **assembly line**. That was a quicker way to make cars. Then you could charge lower prices. This way ordinary people could buy cars. Way to go, Mr. Ford!

Gratefully yours,
Spee D. Kid

post card

Mr. Henry Ford
1863-1947
Dearborn, MI

LAKE SUPERIOR

CANADA

Cool! You can check out old Ford cars in the Legacy Gallery.

LAKE HURON

WISCONSIN

At first, the Ford Rouge Factory made boats. Next, it made tractors. After that, it was cars. Now, the factory makes Ford F-150 trucks.

LAKE MICHIGAN

Detroit
Dearborn

LAKE ERIE

How did the Ford Rouge Factory get its name? It's on the banks of the Rouge River! Rouge is French for "red."

INDIANA

OHIO

THE FORD ROUGE FACTORY IN DEARBORN

Things are really noisy here. Machines are lifting, screwing, and drilling. And look what comes out at the end—a truck!

You're touring the Ford Rouge Factory. Henry Ford opened it in 1917. He was a pioneer in making cars.

People used to travel in horse-drawn carriages. But Ford began thinking about a "horseless carriage." He started the Ford Motor Company in 1903. His Model T cars became very popular. Many car factories opened in southeastern Michigan. Detroit became the nation's car-making center.

You'll see some classic Ford cars on the Ford Rouge Factory tour.

Chug along in a Ford Model T. Ride a steam-powered train. You're in Greenfield Village!

This village spreads out over many acres. It gives you a feel for the past. Farm families are doing their chores. People are making things they need by hand.

One area focuses on Thomas Edison. He invented the phonograph record players and many other things. You'll explore his workshop and see his inventions.

Nearby is the Henry Ford Museum. You'll see thousands of machines and everyday items there. They range from airplanes and cars to toasters!

Check out the historic steam-powered train at Greenfield Village.

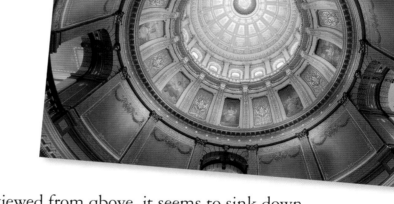

Touring the state capitol is quite a trip. Walk up to the second floor of the building and look down at the rotunda, or the main entrance. The rotunda floor is made of glass. When viewed from above, it seems to sink down like a bowl. But that's just a trick on your eyes. The floor is perfectly flat.

This building houses many state government offices. The state government has three branches. Michigan's governor heads one branch. This branch sees that laws are carried out. Another branch makes laws for the state. Judges make up the third branch. They listen to cases in courts. They decide whether someone has broken the law.

Though they look small, the stars on the capitol's domed ceiling are each the size of your hand.

MOTOWN MUSIC AND DETROIT'S MOTOWN MUSEUM

Remember that city called Motown? It's Detroit, the Motor City. But Detroit is famous for more than cars. It's where Motown music was born!

Motown music was created in 1959. It's an African American music style. It combines gospel, soul, and rhythm and blues. Smokey Robinson and the Miracles were big Motown stars. So were The Supremes and The Temptations.

People all over the country loved Motown music. Motown opened the door for many African American musicians. Want to learn all about Motown and its stars? Visit the Motown Museum in Detroit!

Learn more about the history of Motown music at Detroit's Motown Museum.

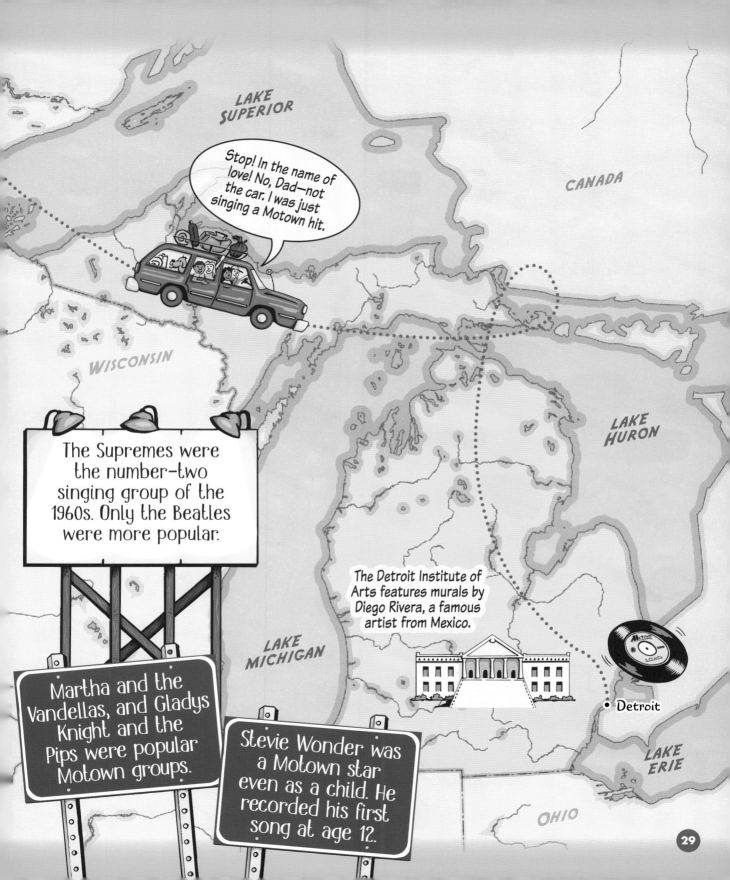

Stop! In the name of love! No, Dad—not the car. I was just singing a Motown hit.

The Supremes were the number-two singing group of the 1960s. Only the Beatles were more popular.

Martha and the Vandellas, and Gladys Knight and the Pips were popular Motown groups.

The Detroit Institute of Arts features murals by Diego Rivera, a famous artist from Mexico.

Stevie Wonder was a Motown star even as a child. He recorded his first song at age 12.

What Are Michigan's Fishing Products?
Whitefish, salmon, and lake trout

Both Traverse City and Eau Claire hold cherry festivals in July.

CANADA

Escanaba •

The Upper Peninsula State Fair is held in mid-August in Escanaba. The Michigan State Fair is held in Novi in early September.

LAKE HURON

• Traverse City

WISCONSIN

Oh, boy! They have a kids' division. Pucker up and aim high!

LAKE MICHIGAN

Novi •

What Does Michigan Raise? Milk, greenhouse and nursery products, soybeans, and corn

Eau Claire

Approximately three million Christmas trees are grown in Michigan each year.

EAU CLAIRE'S CHERRY PIT SPITTING CHAMPIONSHIP

Thwit! Thwit! Thwit! Stand back. It's the International Cherry Pit Spitting Championship!

This may seem like a silly contest. But the spitters are very serious. They get three chances to spit. What if they swallow a cherry pit? Then they lose that turn!

Michigan is a leading state in growing cherries. Its rich soil is good for raising many crops. Corn is the leading field crop. Farmers also grow wheat, hay, and soybeans.

Many Michigan farmers grow flowers and shrubs. One Michigan crop is very popular in December. It's Christmas trees!

A scientist examines a cherry tree in Michigan to make sure it's free from pests.

THE W. K. KELLOGG MANOR HOUSE IN HICKORY CORNERS

Do you like Kellogg's Corn Flakes? Would you like to learn about one of the inventors of this cereal? If so, then the W. K. Kellogg Manor House in Hickory Corners is a must-see site. This manor was W. K. Kellogg's summer home. W. K. and his brother, John H. Kellogg, invented toasted corn flakes.

W. K.'s manor was built in the 1920s. There are many fun places to explore on the manor grounds. You'll find a rose garden, a greenhouse, and even an island with an old Dutch windmill.

The Kellogg Company helped establish cereal production as a top industry in Michigan. Both Post and Kellogg's cereals got their start there. Battle Creek makes more cereal than any other city in the world.

Workers maintain the grounds of the W. K. Kellogg Manor House.

The Battle Creek Toasted Corn Flake Company opened in 1906.

What's Made in Michigan? Transportation equipment, machinery, metal products, and chemicals

Let's check out the Sojourner Truth Monument in Battle Creek. Sojourner Truth spoke out against slavery in the 1800s.

LAKE SUPERIOR

LAKE HURON

WISCONSIN

LAKE MICHIGAN

W. K. Kellogg formed the W. K. Kellogg Foundation in 1930. It supports children's health and education.

Hickory Corners • • Battle Creek

What's Mined in Michigan? Natural gas, iron ore, and petroleum

The Underground Railroad Sculpture in Battle Creek honors men and women who helped African Americans escape slavery.

LAKE ERIE

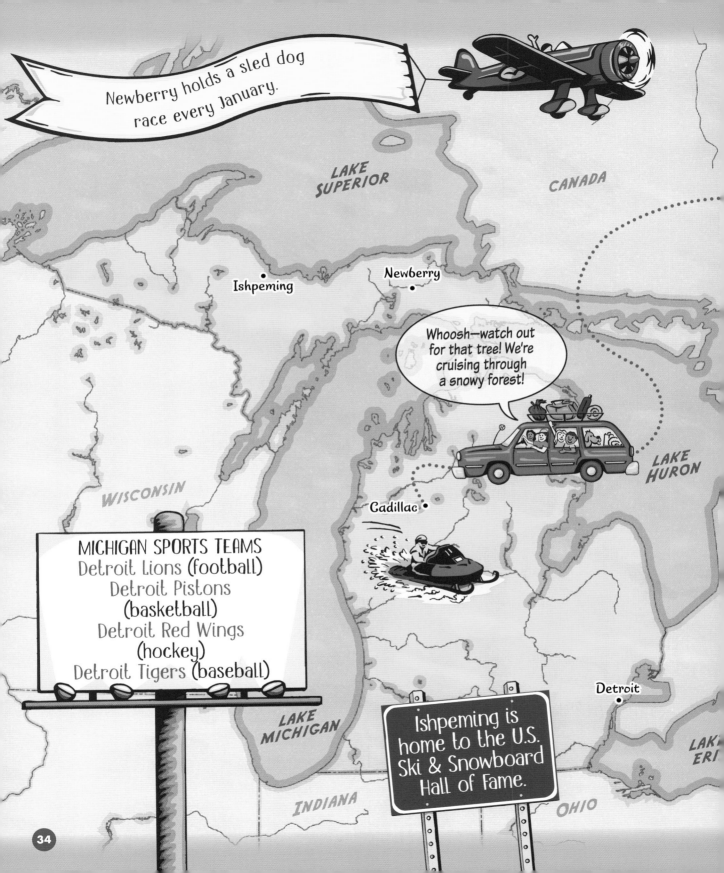

Newberry holds a sled dog race every January.

LAKE SUPERIOR

CANADA

Ishpeming

Newberry

Whoosh—watch out for that tree! We're cruising through a snowy forest!

LAKE HURON

WISCONSIN

Cadillac

MICHIGAN SPORTS TEAMS
Detroit Lions (football)
Detroit Pistons (basketball)
Detroit Red Wings (hockey)
Detroit Tigers (baseball)

Detroit

LAKE MICHIGAN

Ishpeming is home to the U.S. Ski & Snowboard Hall of Fame.

LAKE ERIE

INDIANA

OHIO

THE NORTH AMERICAN SNOW FESTIVAL IN CADILLAC

The racers zoom through jumps, twists, and turns. Swoosh! They reach the finish line. You're watching a snowmobile race at the North American Snow Festival. Want to try it yourself? No problem. They have kids' races, too.

Snowmobiling is a big sport in Michigan. People love snowmobiling through snowy forests. They whip around trees and rumble over logs. Snow skiing and ice skating are popular, too. When it's warmer, people enjoy hiking and camping. Some take canoes down the rivers. Others like fishing in the clear streams.

There's a lot to do along the lakeshores, too. You can climb sand dunes. Then sit down and slide to the bottom. Whee!

Cadillac is a popular snowmobiling destination because it gets lots of snow in winter.

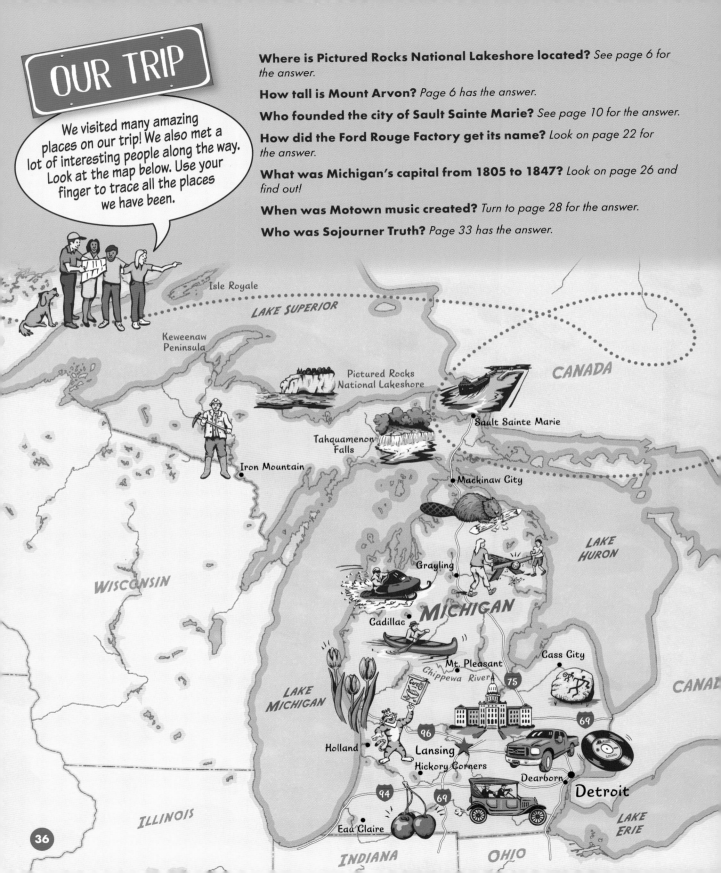

OUR TRIP

We visited many amazing places on our trip! We also met a lot of interesting people along the way. Look at the map below. Use your finger to trace all the places we have been.

Where is Pictured Rocks National Lakeshore located? *See page 6 for the answer.*

How tall is Mount Arvon? *Page 6 has the answer.*

Who founded the city of Sault Sainte Marie? *See page 10 for the answer.*

How did the Ford Rouge Factory get its name? *Look on page 22 for the answer.*

What was Michigan's capital from 1805 to 1847? *Look on page 26 and find out!*

When was Motown music created? *Turn to page 28 for the answer.*

Who was Sojourner Truth? *Page 33 has the answer.*

Isle Royale

LAKE SUPERIOR

Keweenaw Peninsula

CANADA

Pictured Rocks National Lakeshore

Sault Sainte Marie

Tahquamenon Falls

Iron Mountain

Mackinaw City

WISCONSIN

LAKE HURON

Grayling

MICHIGAN

Cadillac

Cass City

LAKE MICHIGAN

Mt. Pleasant

Chippewa River

75

CANADA

Holland

96

69

Lansing

Hickory Corners

Dearborn

Detroit

94

69

LAKE ERIE

ILLINOIS

Eau Claire

INDIANA

OHIO

STATE SYMBOLS

State bird: American robin

State fish: Brook trout

State flower: Apple blossom

State game mammal: White-tailed deer

State gem: Chlorastrolite

State reptile: Painted turtle

State soil: Kalkaska sand

State stone: Petoskey stone

State tree: White pine

State wildflower: Dwarf lake iris

State flag

That was a great trip! We have traveled all over Michigan! There are a few places that we didn't have time for, though. Next time, we plan to visit the Ambassador Bridge in Detroit. This bridge connects two countries. It stretches over the Detroit River between the United States and Windsor, Canada. It was built in 1929.

STATE SONG

"MICHIGAN, MY MICHIGAN"

For many years, people thought Michigan had no official state song. But recently, the Michigan Historical Center discovered "My Michigan," with words by Giles Kavanagh and music by H. O'Reilly Clint. "My Michigan" was made an official state song in 1937. But "Michigan, My Michigan" has long been considered the unofficial state song and is still the popular choice in patriotic programs throughout the state. Winifred Lee Brent wrote the first version in 1862. Douglas Malloch wrote new words in 1902. His version is used today.

A song to thee, fair State of mine,
Michigan, my Michigan;
But greater song than this is thine,
Michigan, my Michigan;
The whisper of the forest tree,
The thunder of the inland sea;
Unite in one grand symphony
Of Michigan, my Michigan.

I sing a State of all the best,
Michigan, my Michigan;
I sing a State with riches blest,
Michigan, my Michigan;
Thy mines unmask a hidden store,
But richer thy historic lore,
More great the love thy builders bore,
Oh, Michigan, my Michigan.

How fair the bosom of thy lakes,
Michigan, my Michigan;
What melody each river makes,
Michigan, my Michigan;
As to thy lakes the rivers tend,
Thy exiled children to thee send
Devotion that shall never end,
Oh, Michigan, my Michigan.
Thou rich in wealth that makes a State,
Michigan, my Michigan;
Thou great in things that make us great,
Michigan, my Michigan;
Our loyal voices sound they claim
Upon the golden roll of fame
Our loyal hands shall write the name
Of Michigan, my Michigan.

FAMOUS PEOPLE

Bell, Kristen (1980–), actor

Boeing, William E. (1881–1956), aircraft company founder

Coppola, Francis Ford (1939–), film director

Curtis, Christopher Paul (1953–), children's author

Eminem (1972–), rapper

Ford, Gerald (1913–2006), 28th U.S. president

Ford, Henry (1863–1947), inventor, automobile manufacturer

Franklin, Aretha (1942–), singer

Gipp, George "the Gipper" (1895–1920), football player

Johnson, Earvin "Magic" (1959–), basketball player

Lautner, Taylor (1992–), actor

Lindbergh, Charles A. (1902–1974), pilot, Pulitzer Prize winner

Madonna (1958–), singer

Moore, Michael (1954–), documentary filmmaker and author

Polacco, Patricia (1944–), children's author and illustrator

Quimby, Harriet (ca. 1875–1912), first licensed American woman pilot

Robinson, Sugar Ray (1921–1989), boxer

Truth, Sojourner (ca. 1797–1883), abolitionist and women's rights activist

Van Allsburg, Chris (1949-), children's author and illustrator

Wonder, Stevie (1950–), singer

WORDS TO KNOW

ancestors (AN-sess-turz) grandparents, great-grandparents, and earlier relatives

assembly line (uh-SEM-blee LINE) a line of workers and machines that repeat the same actions to produce a product

canal (kuh-NAL) a waterway dug by people

convert (kuhn-VURT) to change something such as a person's religion or beliefs

immigrants (IM-uh-gruhntz) people who move from their home country to a new land

industry (IN-duh-stree) a type of business

ore (OR) rock that is filled with a metal

peninsula (puh-NIN-suh-luh) land almost completely surrounded by water

pioneers (pye-uh-NEERZ) people who move into a place where no one has settled before

straits (STRAYTZ) narrow waterways that connect two large bodies of water

traditional (truh-DISH-uhn-uhl) following long-held customs

State seal

TO LEARN MORE

IN THE LIBRARY

Niver, Heather Moore. *Sojourner Truth*. New York, NY: Gareth Stevens, 2015.

Pinkney, Andrea Davis. *Rhythm Ride: A Road Trip through the Motown Sound*.
New York, NY: Roaring Brook, 2015.

Ramsey, Torren. *Ojibwe*. New York, NY: PowerKids, 2016.

Rechner, Amy. *Michigan: The Great Lakes State*. Minneapolis, MN: Bellwether, 2014.

ON THE WEB

Visit our Web site for links about Michigan:
childsworld.com/links

*Note to Parents, Teachers, and Librarians: We routinely verify our Web links to make sure
they are safe and active sites. So encourage your readers to check them out!*

PLACES TO VISIT OR CONTACT
Michigan History Center
michigan.gov/mhc
702 W. Kalamazoo Street
Lansing, MI 48915
517/373-3559
For more information about the history of Michigan

Travel Michigan
michigan.org
300 N. Washington Square
Lansing, MI 48913
517/335-4590
For more information about traveling in Michigan

Michigan covers 96,714 square miles (250,488 sq km). It's the 11th-largest state in size.

INDEX

Bye, Wolverine State. We had a great time. We'll come back soon!